■ SCHOLASTIC

Best of Dr. Jean

Reading & Writing

More Than 100 Delightful, Skill-Building Ideas and Activities for Early Learners

by Dr. Jean Feldman

Oral Language & Vocabulary

Phonemic Awareness

Letter Knowledge

Concepts of Print

NEW YORK • TORONTO • LONDON • AUCKLAND • SYDNEY
MEXICO CITY • NEW DELHI • HONG KONG • BUENOS AIRES

Teaching *Resources*

To Mrs. Myers, my kindergarten and first-grade teacher

She made me feel special and she made coming to school
the most exciting thing in my life!

My wish is that the activities in this book will instill
the same love of learning in your students!

Cover illustration by Brenda Sexton
Cover and interior design by Holly Grundon
Interior illustration by Milk and Cookies

ISBN: 0-439-59726-9
Copyright © 2005 by Dr. Jean Feldman
Published by Scholastic Inc.

1 2 3 4 5 6 7 8 9 10   40   13 12 11 10 09 08 07 06 05

Contents

Introduction

Welcome to Best of Dr. Jean
Reading & Writing

This book is about much more than teaching letters and words. It's about building a love of letters, words, and language. It's about creating lifelong readers. It's about helping children fall in love with language, books, and learning! The games, books, rhymes, songs, and activities in this book are based on research, but they are also fun. When materials and activities are interesting, engaging, playful, and fun, children will want to "do it again"!

Research-Based

As early childhood teachers, the more we know about the latest research in reading and brain development, the better we will be at validating what we know is best for young children! All the things you and your children already love—reading, singing, talking, playing, creating—are in the research. Know that what you are doing is appropriate and effective, believe in what you are doing, and share the good news from the research with administrators and parents.

Best practices recommended by the International Reading Association (see page 5) include building a class community, working with children in small groups, giving children time to read and write, using high-quality literature, and integrating a word study/phonics program into reading instruction. We can all aspire to employ these best practices daily in their classroom!

Highlights from an extensive review of the research by the National Association for the Education of Young Children (see page 5) recommend:

* reading aloud to children
* creating a print-rich environment
* promoting oral language and vocabulary
* developing phonemic awareness
* exposing children to rhymes, traditional songs, and name games
* developing alphabet knowledge
* helping children develop strategies for decoding words
* integrating reading and writing
* providing children with books

Literacy Centers

Many of the activities in this book are designed for centers. In addition to the traditional reading and writing centers (see page 6), you can infuse literacy into almost any area of the room (see page 7)! In centers, children might work independently, with a partner, or in a small group.

So much happens when you integrate literacy into your centers. Take a look at the skills you'll be building:

✳ print awareness	✳ phonics	✳ cooperation
✳ letter knowledge	✳ independence	✳ sharing
✳ reading fluency	✳ motivation	✳ oral language

Meeting the Standards

The activities in this book align with the guidelines and recommended teaching practices set out by the National Association for the Education of Young Children and the International Reading Association (1998):

Recommended teaching practices:

✳ share books with children and model reading behaviors

✳ talk about letters by name and sounds

✳ establish a literacy-rich environment

✳ reread favorite stories

✳ engage children in language games

✳ promote literacy-related play activities

✳ encourage children to experiment with writing

Young children need developmentally appropriate experiences and teaching to support literacy learning. To this end, teachers can provide:

✳ positive, nurturing relationships with adults who engage in responsive conversations with children, model reading and writing behavior, and foster children's interest in and enjoyment of reading and writing;

✳ print-rich environments that provide opportunities and tools for children to see and use written language for a variety of purposes, with teachers drawing children's attention to specific letters and words;

✳ adults' daily reading of high-quality books to individuals or small groups, including books that positively reflect children's identity, home language, and culture;

✳ opportunities for children to talk about what is read and to focus on the sounds and parts of language as well as the meaning;

✳ teaching strategies and experiences that develop phonemic awareness, such as songs, fingerplays, games, poems, and stories in which phonemic patterns such as rhyme and alliteration are salient;

✳ opportunities to engage in play that incorporates literacy tools, such as writing grocery lists in dramatic play, making signs in block building, and using icons and words in exploring a computer game; and

✳ firsthand experiences that expand children's vocabulary, such as trips in the community and exposure to various tools, objects, and materials.

Source: Learning to Read and Write: Developmentally Appropriate Practices for Young Children © 1998 by the National Association for the Education of Young Children.

Materials for a **Reading Center**

- picture books
- interactive books
- collaborative class books
- book bags
- headphones & player with tapes or CDs
- flannel board & felt pieces
- leveled books
- maps

- catalogs
- magazines
- brochures
- menus
- posters
- puppets & stuffed animals to read to
- pillows
- beanbag chairs
- rocking chair
- whisper phones*

And...

- Create a "cool reading pool" with an old plastic swimming pool, pillows, a quilt, and stuffed animals.
- Let children decorate an appliance box to become a "reading clubhouse."

Materials for a **Writing Center**

- pens & pencils
- crayons
- markers
- colored pencils
- colored paper
- blank paper
- lined paper
- notepads
- notebooks
- office stationery
- blank checkbooks
- carbon paper
- envelopes

- junk mail
- stamps & nontoxic ink pad
- chalkboard
- dry erase board & markers
- magic slate
- clipboard
- scissors
- hole punch
- tape
- glue
- stapler

- dictionary
- picture file
- Rolodex
- magnetic letters
- computer
- printer
- manual typewriter
- blank books

And...

- An old desk would be a great attraction!

---

* See page 12.

Creating Literacy-Rich
Learning Centers

Add these materials to the other learning centers in your classroom to encourage children to read and write in meaningful ways:

Math Center
* paper
* pens & pencils
* adding machine tape
* coupons
* calculator
* play money
* graphs
* posters
* counting books
* shape books

Science Center
* nonfiction books on science topics
* science magazines
* labeled pictures of animals, plants, flowers, and so on
* clipboard
* pens & pencils
* notebooks

Dramatic Play Center
* shopping list
* chalkboard
* memo pad
* pens & pencils

* magazines
* books
* puppets
* stuffed animals & dolls to read to
* junk mail
* menus
* catalogs
* class phone book

Block Center
* paper & markers to make labels & signs
* sticky notes
* photos of different homes & buildings
* maps & blueprints
* alphabet blocks

Art Center
* rebus direction charts or cards
* labels for materials
* variety of art media
* markers
* paint

Fine-Motor Table
* play dough

* letter cookie cutters
* play dough book
* sewing cards
* letter beads to string
* paper
* hole punch
* scissors
* letter stencils
* colored pencils

Sand and Water Center
* magnetic letters (to hide in sand)
* Ping-Pong balls (write letters and words on them and have children scoop them from the water with a fishnet)
* craft sticks (to write in sand)

Playground
* beach balls (print on letters with permanent marker)
* chalk & chalkboard for keeping score
* sidewalk chalk

Authentic Literacy Activities

Authentic literacy experiences show children that print serves important purposes. Have children participate in the activities below frequently to:

* Make the connection between spoken word and print
* Build small-motor skills
* Integrate reading and writing
* Build alphabet knowledge

* Develop print awareness
* Build confidence
* Recognize the importance of reading and writing
* Develop oral language

Sign-In Chart
Invite children to sign their name on a piece of butcher paper or chart paper when they enter the classroom each day.

Take a Turn
Have children use sign-up sheets to work on the computer, play in a center, take home a collaborative book, and so on.

Rights & Responsibilities Chart
At the beginning of the year, make a list of classroom expectations. When children are behaving inappropriately, point to the appropriate text and read it aloud as you remind them what to do.

Sticky Notes
Keep sticky notes handy for reminders, thank yous, and so on. You can stick them right to children's clothes!

Daily Schedule
Post a daily schedule (illustrated with photos or pictures from school catalogs) and review it with children every day.

Morning Message
On chart paper, write a message about special activities each morning before children arrive at school.

Classroom Concerns Notebook
Set out a notebook in which children can write comments or concerns. (This is great for children who tattle!)

Message Center
Set out dry erase or chalkboard for children to write notes to each other with markers or chalk.

Labels and Signs
Make labels with pictures so children know where toys and classroom materials should be stored. You might use pictures cut from school supply catalogs.

Phonemic Awareness

Being able to recognize the different sounds that make up spoken language is a key element in literacy development. These activities build that awareness with rhythm, rhyme, and word-play.

Gumball Sounds

Have fun with alliteration!

Materials: none

How To:

1. Sing the song at right to the tune of "Good Night, Ladies." Use initial consonant substitution to alliterate the phrases.

2. Continue, substituting other consonant sounds.

And...

✳ When a child has a birthday, sing the birthday song by "alliterating" every word with the sound that begins his or her name!

✳ Say familiar nursery rhymes and other songs by alliterating beginning sounds. For example: *Bumpty bumpty bat on a ball. Bumpty bumpty bad a breat ball...*

✳ Say this chant about "Pepperoni Pizza." Substitute a different vowel sound each time you repeat it!

I like to eat, eat, eat pepperoni pizza.
I like to eat, eat, eat pepperoni pizza.

Long -a sound:
A lake tay ate, ate, ate papparanay pizzay.
A lake tay ate, ate, ate papparanay pizzay.
Continue with /ē/, /ī/, /ō/, and /ū/.

> I put a penny in the gum slot.
> I watched the gum roll down.
> I get the gum and you get the wrapper,
> 'Cause I put the penny in the gum slot.
>
> Now put a /b/ in front of each word.
> Bi but a benny bin be bum bot.
> Bi batched be bum boll bown.
> Bi bet be bum band bou bet ba bapper,
> Bause bi but ba benny bin be bum bot.
>
> Now try the /n/ sound.
> Ni nut a nenny nin ne num not...

Rhyme Farm

Build listening and critical-thinking skills as you help kids develop phonological awareness.

Materials: none

How To:

Read the riddles below and on page 11 to children. Explain that the answer will rhyme. Practice rhyming words to get children warmed up (*red, bed, fed*).

I give you milk.
Do you want some now?
I say, "Moo moo."
I'm a _____.

I have horns
and a beard on my throat.
"Naa-naa-naa!"
I'm a _____.

In the dirt,
I play and dig.
"Oink, oink, oink!"
I am a _____.

"Cluck, cluck, cluck,"
I lay eggs in the pen,
because I am a pretty
_____.

I'll give you a ride
on my back, of course.
"Neigh, neigh, neigh!"
I'm a _____.

Who would like
My wool to keep?
"Baa-baa-baa."
I'm a _____.

Rhyme Farm

I can be white or black
Skinny or fat.
"Meow, meow, meow!"
I'm a _____.

In "Little Miss Muffet,"
I sat down beside her.
I can spin webs.
I'm a _____.

You always swat me.
I don't know why!
"Zzzz! Zzzz! Zzzz!"
I'm a _____.

When it rains,
I'm in luck.
"Quack, quack!"
I'm a _____.

I'm your best friend.
I'm not a hog!
"Woof! Woof! Woof!"
I'm a _____.

"Tweet-tweet-tweet"
are my sweet words.
I fly all around.
I'm a _____.

And...

✳ Set out plastic farm animals (or pictures of them) and let children
select the one that answers the riddle.

✳ Say a series of three words and have children select the two that
rhyme. For example: *kitten, house, mitten* or *log, hog, car*.

✳ Share other riddle books and joke books with children. Have a
"Comedy Circle" in which children stand up and tell jokes and
riddles to their classmates.

Phonemic Awareness

Phonics Phones

Also called "whisper phones," these devices amplify children's voices. They're great for independent work at centers, building reading confidence, and helping children really hear the sounds they are decoding.

Materials: two one-inch PVC elbows, one two-inch section of PVC pipe (one inch in diameter)

How To:

1. Insert the section of PVC pipe between the two elbows to make a "phone."

2. Hold the phone to your mouth and demonstrate how to whisper into it. Use it for any of these activities (pages 12–13).

Alliteration

Have children repeat a sound and a corresponding alliterative phrase (for instance, short e: *Elmo enjoys eggs*).

Rhyme

Invite children to repeat nursery rhymes or a series of words that rhyme.

Syllables

Have children slowly say words and identify how many syllables are in each word.

Separate Sounds

Separate individual phonemes in words, such as /c/ /a/ /t/. Children like to call this "word stretching"!

Independent Reading

Children simply listen to themselves as they read aloud.

Invented Spelling

Children say a word slowly and write the sounds they hear. This is great for journal writing.

Telephone Switchboard

Tie one end of an old phone cord around the whisper phone. Use duct tape to attach the other end of the cord to a file folder on which you have written each letter of the alphabet. Children put the whisper phone to their ears, close their eyes, put their finger down on the folder, open their eyes, then reproduce the sound on which they landed.

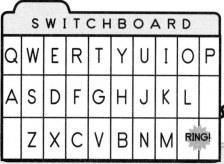

And...

✳ For health reasons, children should each have his or her own phone.

✳ Clean the phones frequently by running them in a dishwasher.

✳ If you don't have phonics phones, show children how to make a "hand phone" by cupping one hand behind an ear and the other hand around the mouth.

✳ Give children hand mirrors so they can observe their lips and tongues as they reproduce different sounds.

Letter Knowledge

The ability to recognize, identify, and form letters, as well as associate them with their sounds, is key to literacy development. Whether you are teaching uppercase letters, lowercase letters, or both, these activities will build letter recognition skills as well as children's interest in print.

Invisible Writing

By adding large movements to letter writing, it will be easier for children to remember the strokes involved in each letter's formation.

Materials: none

How To:

1. Have children stand (face away from them so that you will demonstrate the letter correctly). Raise your index finger, middle finger and keep your elbow stiff.

2. Slowly write a letter in the air as you explain the strokes you're demonstrating. For instance, *Slant down. Slant down. Connect them in the middle to make an A.* Erase each letter by "swishing" your hand in the air!

3. Have children try it themselves. Children can also do "invisible writing" on the palms of their hands or on each other's backs. They can also write on the floor with their feet!

And...

✳ To enhance cross-lateral learning, use the left and right hand at the same time as you do invisible writing.

✳ Use invisible writing for making shapes, numerals, words, or anything else you're working on.

✳ Give children a wet sponge and let them write letters on the chalkboard using large strokes. The letters will slowly disappear as the water evaporates. This is also a great way to clean the chalkboards!

Giant Keyboard

Build gross-motor and letter-recognition skills at the same time!

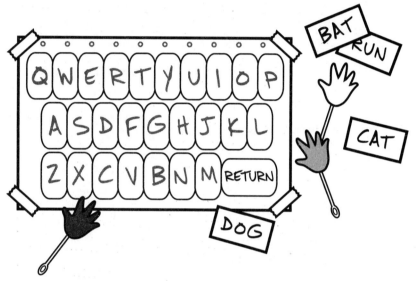

Materials: shower curtain liner, flyswatter, permanent marker

How To:

1. In advance, cut a shower curtain in half lengthwise. Lay it out on the floor and draw out a keyboard. Cut the flyswatter so that it resembles a hand or mitten. Attach the keyboard to a wall.

2. With the flyswatter, "swat" letters and spell out words as children identify them. Then let individual children have turns swatting!

And...

✳ Let children work with the giant keyboard in pairs. One child holds up a sight word or spelling word on an index card. His or her partner "types" out the word with the flyswatter. Children take turns typing and checking each other.

✳ Remind children to hit the "return" button when they've completed a word.

✳ Divide the class into two teams and give each a different color flyswatter. One child from each team takes a flyswatter and stands to the side of the keyboard, then you call out a letter. The first child to swat that letter gets a point for his or her team. Children take turns being the "swatter"!

Eight Little Letters

Get physical learners involved with letter recognition as you focus on commonly confused letters.

Materials: eight file folders (in different colors if possible), marker, hole punch, string

How To:

1. In advance, cut folders in half along the fold. Punch holes in the top of each half and thread through a 24-inch piece of string. Tie to make a "sandwich board" or vest children can wear. Write the lowercase letter on the front and the uppercase letter on the back for these letters: n, m, t, f, g, d, s, p. (Put a sticker on the side with the lowercase letter so children will know to wear it in front.)

2. Choose eight children to wear the file folders. Have children show off their letters and invite children to name them, identifying upper- and lowercase as the wearers turn around.

3. After they have named the eight letters and made their sounds, ask the whole group to walk in a circle as you sing this song to the tune of "Five Little Ducks:"

Eight little letters went out one day
(*Hold up eight fingers.*)

Over the hills and far away.
(*Move hands up and down.*)

When the teacher called /m/, /m/, /m/, /m/ (*Cup hands by mouth.*)

Only the letter M came back.
(*Make /m/ sound. The child wearing the m sits in the middle of the circle.*)

Continue with /n/, /t/, /f/, /g/, /d/, /s/, and /p/.

And...

❋ Try this with vowels, blends, or digraphs.

❋ If you have 26 children in your group, have children wear letter vests for all 26 letters. Call out different letters and have children come up, hold hands, and make words!

❋ Use the letters to demonstrate onset and rime (chunking). Have children wearing *a* and *t* stand together to form *at*. Have different children come up with their letter and stand in front of *at* to make *rat, fat, bat, mat, sat,* and so on.

❋ Say a word very slowly, clearly enunciating each sound. If children hear the sound of their letter, they come up to the front of the group and make the word.

Finger Spelling

Here's an all-time favorite!

Materials: three pairs of cloth garden gloves (two in one color, one in a different color), black permanent marker

How To:

1. In advance, cut the fingers off the gloves. Write a lowercase consonant on the fingers of one color glove. Write lowercase vowels on the fingers of the other color glove. (Write the same letter on the front and back of each finger.)

2. Demonstrate how to put the letters on your fingers to spell a word. Make the sound for each letter as you do so; then, as a group, blend the sounds to make a word.

And...

✳ Demonstrate "magic fingers." Change one letter at a time to make different words, such as *cat, bat, bit, big, pig*.

✳ Make nonsense words as well as real ones (children like to call the nonsense words "alien" words)!

✳ Have children use finger letters to show word families.

✳ Use to reinforce high-frequency words.

Letter Knowledge

Sing & Sign

Introduce sign language by singing this song to the tune of "Where Is Thumbkin?"

Materials: none

How To:

1. Sing:

   Where is A?
   (Hands behind back.)

   Where is A?
   (Children repeat.)

   Here I am.
   (With your hand, make sign for a.)

   Here I am.
   (Children repeat and mimic sign.)

   What do you say, A?
   (Wiggle sign for a.)

   What do you say, A?
   (Children repeat.)

   /a/, /a/, /a/.
   (Make short-a sound.)

   /a/, /a/, /a/.
   (Children repeat short-a sound.)

2. Repeat, using other letters.

And...

✳ Teach each child the sign for the first letter of his or her name. For a silent transition to line up or dismiss children, simply make the different signs.

✳ Spell out high-frequency words in sign language.

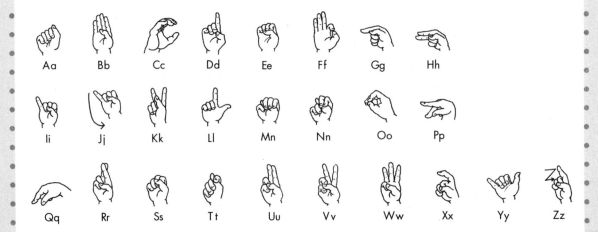

Letter Land

Involve children in making one of these meaningful alphabets to display in the classroom.

Materials: poster board, large index cards, markers, crayons, glue, photographs, pictures, and other art supplies

Photo Alphabet

Write a letter of the alphabet on each of 26 sheets of heavy paper. Glue on photos of children whose names start with each letter. (You can use first or last names.) Have children print their names at the bottom. Let children decide what to do for letters without names! (They might think of characters in books or movies.) Display as an alphabet frieze.

The Real ABCs

Glue real objects that begin with each letter onto sheets of heavy paper. For instance, Aa *is for acorn,* Bb *is for a bit of branch.* Cc *is for crayon,* and so on. Display as a frieze.

Giant ABCs

Cut out large letters from construction paper or poster board. Give children each a letter to take home and decorate with their families. Challenge them to use materials whose names begin with that sound (for instance, colored sand for S), or to cut out pictures of objects that begin with the sound to create a collage. You might also focus on one letter at a time and do this as a class project.

Environmental Print

Assign each child a letter and have children look through old magazines to find several examples of the letter (the larger, the better) and cut them out. Glue their findings in alphabetical order onto poster board, or glue each onto a separate sheet of heavy paper.

Name Games

Kids love recognizing their own names — and the names of their classmates!

Materials: a photo of each child, sentence strips, markers, basket or box

How To:

1. Make a name card for each child by printing his or her first and last name on a sentence strip.

2. Glue his or her photograph onto the strip.

3. Store the name cards in a box or basket and use them for any of the activities below.

Syllables

Clap out each child's name to determine the number of syllables.

Alliteration

Think of an adjective that begins with the first letter of each child's name (Kind Kara, Awesome Alan, and so on).

Letters

Count the letters in each child's name. Who has the most? Fewest? Graph the results.

Sound Alike

Sort names into piles: *Whose first names begin with the same sound? Whose last names begin the same?*

Rhymes

Change the first letter of children's names to make silly rhymes (Jamey/Wamey, Pablo/Wablo, Jenny/Penny, and so on).

Sign In

Have children find their name in the basket and use it as a model to write their name when they sign in each day.

Writing Center

Store cards in the writing center for children to refer to if they want to include classmates' names in their writing.

Transitions

Pick names for the order in which children should line up, go to a center, get their backpacks, and so on.

Helpers

Pick names at random to choose a special helper, decide which child to call on, and so on.

Cheer

Cheer children's names. *(Give me a T—T! Give me an A—A! Give me a D—D! What's it spell? Tad! Say it again. Tad! One more time! Tad!)*

Hickety Pickety Bumbleebee

Clap, snap, or slap the beat!

Hickety pickety bumbleebee,

Who can say their name for me?

(Hold up name card. That child says name.)

(Class repeats name.)

Clap it. *(Clap syllables in name.)*

Snap it. *(Snap syllables.)*

Whisper it.
(Whisper name with distinct syllables.)

No sound. *(Mouth name.)*

(Continue holding up name cards and clapping, snapping, and whispering.)

Pup, Pup, What's Up?

This letter-recognition game has a built-in self-check.

Materials: construction paper, markers, scissors

How To:

1. Cut simple puppy shapes out of construction paper using the pattern below. Bend down the ear and draw on a mouth, an eye, and a nose.

2. Write a lowercase letter on the puppy's body; then lift the ear and write the uppercase letter underneath.

3. Children identify letters, visualize their uppercase form, then self-check by lifting the ear.

And...

✳ Put pictures on the puppy and the corresponding beginning sounds under its ear.

Woof! Woof!

Children will "eat up" this exercise!

Materials: plastic bowl, scissors, construction paper, markers

How To:

1. Cut 26 dog bones from construction paper. Write a different letter on each bone. Put the bones in the "dog bowl."

2. Pass the bowl around and have each child choose a bone and identify the letter on it. Ask each child to make the sound the letter makes, then think of a word that begins with that sound.

And...

✳ Cut out 25 bones and write high-frequency words on 22 of them. Write "WOOF!" on the other three bones. Place the bones in the dog bowl. Pass the bowl around the room. Children select a bone and read the word on it. If they select one that says "WOOF!" they stand up and bark like a dog!

Magnetic Letters

Try any or all of these magnetic ideas!

Materials: assortment of magnetic letters, jumbo craft sticks, glue, metal cookie sheet, magnet

✳ Place the letters on a table. Have each child find the letter that begins his or her name.

✳ Glue magnetic letters to jumbo craft sticks. Children can use these to match letters on print they see around the classroom. They can also take letter sticks and find something in the room beginning with that sound.

✳ Demonstrate how to build words with magnetic letters. (This is really neat on the overhead projector!)

✳ Use magnetic letters on a cookie sheet or file cabinet. What a fun way for children to make word families!

✳ Hide magnetic letters in your sand table. Children can hold a magnet and try to identify letters that they attract.

✳ Place several letters you are working on around the door frame. As children leave the room, ask them to touch the letter they hear at the beginning of any given word.

Alphabet Books

Children love creating their own ABC books and want to
read them again and again. Try any of these ideas on pages 24–27.

Sweet ABCs

Have children bring in candy
wrappers. Take 26 sheets of paper,
write a different letter on each
page, and put the pages between
two sheets of construction paper to
make a book. Hole-punch and bind
with yarn. Children take their
wrappers and glue them on the
page with the matching beginning
sound (for instance, M: M&M's.)
Write silly comments on the pages
that don't have wrappers (for
instance, "H: Help! I need some
candy," "U: Uh-oh! I ate too much
candy!").

Hidden Letters

Scramble the letters of the alphabet on a
page similar to the one below. Make 26
copies. Write "Where is **A**?" with a marker
at the top of the first page, "Where is **B**?"
on the second page, and so on. Bend a pipe
cleaner to look like a magnifying glass. (You
can also use a bubble wand to frame the
letters.) Use construction paper to make
the front and back cover of the book. Hole-
punch and bind the pages with book rings.
Children take the "magnifying glass" and
find the hidden letter on each page. For
younger children, use fewer letters on each
page and limit the number of pages in the
book. You can also make a similar book
with lowercase letters, vocabulary words,
children's names, and so on.

Textured Alphabet Book

On each page, form letters from felt,
sandpaper, yarn, glitter, foam, and so
on. Encourage children to close their
eyes and feel the letters.

Peek a boo

Put a picture for each letter of the alphabet on a different page. (You can cut these from magazines or let children draw them.) Cover the picture with a piece of construction paper and tape it at the top so you can lift and see what the picture is. Write the word for the picture on the construction paper flap. Children try to sound out the word, then "take a peek" to confirm their guess.

Body Letters

Challenge children to make letters of the alphabet with their bodies. Take photographs of them and use these to make an alphabet book. Write the letters on the photos of children's bodies so they can see the correct letter. You might want to let each child make the first letter in his or her name.

T is for

Travis

A B C Camouflage

Write a large letter of the alphabet on a sheet of paper for each child. Challenge them to "camouflage" their letter by turning it into an object, animal, or person. Put their pages together and see if they can find the letter on each page. To make this activity more difficult, ask children to create something out of their letter that begins with the sound their letter makes (for instance, S for snake.)

Alphabet Yearbook

Collect pictures of children, special activities, field trips, parties, themes, etc., throughout the school year. Toward the end of the year, type "A is for . . ." and glue pictures of events and children whose names begin with A on that page. Do a page for each letter of the alphabet. Run off a copy for each child, then let him or her decorate a pocket folder and insert the page to make a personal yearbook. Have an "autograph" party where children collect their friends' signatures.

Magnetic Matchup

1. Write a sentence for each letter of the alphabet on a sheet of paper. For example: "**A** is for _____," "**B** is for _____." Let each child choose a different letter and draw an object for that letter.

2. Encourage the child to write the name of his or her object on the line or dictate it to an adult. Next, place magnetic letters on the copy machine and print a copy of them. Cut apart the letters and have children glue their letter on the page. Put the pages together in alphabetical order and make a front and back cover. As children read the book, ask them to select the actual magnetic letter and hold it up to the page. You can also sing this book to the tune of "Twinkle, Twinkle, Little Star." "A is for alligator. B is for bear. C is for car. D is for doughnut . . ."

Sign Language

Enlarge copies of the sign language alphabet (see page 18). Put a different letter and sign on each page, then let different children draw a picture that begins with that sound. Bind together to make a book. You can also make a book with the Braille alphabet (www.nbp.com). Use white school glue to make the appropriate dots for the Braille letters.

Eat Your Way Through the Alphabet

Assign each child a letter of the alphabet (you might use the first letter of his or her name). On a designated day, ask him or her to bring a snack for the class that begins with that letter. Take a photo of each child with his or her food and write a sentence such as *Owen brought oranges*. Collect pictures and bind to make a book of your yummy memories!

Alphabet Art

Do an art project for each letter of the alphabet. Collect these through the year, then put them together so that each child has an alphabet book he or she will treasure! Here are some activities to try for each letter:

A: Make prints with cut apples and tempera paint.

B: Make prints with wooden blocks and paint.

C: Make a collage from cotton balls!

D: Make pictures using only dots.

E: Create art with an eyedropper and tempera paint.

F: Finger-paint or experiment with fingerprints.

G: Use colored glue to make drawings.

H: Make handprints.

I: Put powdered tempera paint on white paper and use ice as a brush!

J: Drizzle glue onto paper and sprinkle dry Jell-O over it.

K: Cut colored tissue paper into small pieces, paint a thin layer of glue on paper, and lay down shapes to create a "kaleidoscope collage."

L: Make prints with leaves and tempera paint.

M: Make prints with marshmallows and food coloring.

N: Paint on newspaper.

O: Make prints with oranges or onions and tempera paint.

P: Make "point prints"! Use the points of markers only.

Q: Paint with Q-tips

R: Make texture rubbings (place paper over coins) and rub with the side of a crayon.

S: Print with sponges and tempera paint.

T: Make a collage out of torn paper.

U: Draw pictures upside down.

V: Make prints with cut vegetables and tempera paint.

W: Do a watercolor wash. Use crayon on white paper, then paint over it with watercolors.

X: Make an "X marks the spot" treasure map!

Y: Use pieces of yarn as paintbrushes. Dip the yarn into the paint and lay onto paper to make a print.

Z: Cover a sheet of paper with zigzags of every color.

Mystery Letter

Here's a fun way to introduce each letter. Write the letter on white paper with plain school glue. When dry, have children feel it with their fingers and try to guess the letter.

Multisensory Learning

All of these kinesthetic activities provide a unique mode for getting information to the brain and for reinforcing skills.

Lotty Dotty

Make letters and shapes with little dots of glue and let dry. Have children place a sheet of paper on top and rub over it with a crayon. Then, as they connect the dots, they will form the letter!

Scratch & Sniff

Write letters words with glue and sprinkle with dry Jell-O. When it dries, children can touch and sniff!

Texture Writing

Place a sheet of paper over a piece of plastic needlepoint canvas or sandpaper and write letters with crayon.

Rainbow Writing

Have children trace around words, letters, shapes, and so on, using different colored crayons for a rainbow effect.

Roll Out the Letters

Make lines, curves, letters, or words on plastic place mats with a permanent marker. Have children roll out play dough or clay and use it to "trace" the lines and letters. (See page 29 for a complete description.)

Rub Overs

On thick paper or cardboard, write letters or words using colored glue and let dry. Place a sheet of paper on top of the glue and rub over with the side of a crayon. (You can also write with a water-soluble marker and trace over with school glue.)

Concepts of Print

Understanding that print carries meaning, that we read from left to right and top to bottom, that a book has a front cover and a back cover—all are aspects of print awareness. Support children's growing recognition of characteristics and conventions of written language with these activities.

Skill Books

Develop small-motor skills while giving children the opportunity to practice the basic strokes used in printing.

Materials: file folders, markers, hole punch, book rings, laminating sheets, play dough or clay

How To:

1. In advance, take four file folders and draw straight lines, curves, circles, and other shapes (one per sheet) with a marker. Laminate, hole-punch, and bind with book rings.
2. Place the book on a table with some play dough or clay.
3. Children roll, mold, and form the dough or clay to fit on the figures on each page.

Story Symbols

**Reinforce the concept of left-right, top-bottom directionality
as well as the concept of beginning and end.**

Materials: paper (one sheet per child), crayons, rulers, pencils, chart paper, markers

How To:

1. Give each child a sheet of paper and crayons.

2. Demonstrate on chart paper how to draw a green line down the left side of the paper. Say, *Green means GO! We'll always start at the green line.* Demonstrate how to draw a red line down the right side. Say, *Red means STOP! We'll always stop when we get to the red line.*

3. Explain that children will use their crayons to tell a story. Model the strokes below as you go. Say, *First, let's walk to the zoo. Put your crayon on the green line at the top of your page. Walk it across your paper. When you get to the red line, stop. Go back to the green line. There are some ducks swimming. Make your crayon swim across the page!*

4. Continue telling the story at the bottom of the page as children make the symbols. When you are finished, challenge children to retell the story by looking at the symbols.

And...

* Use the overhead to demonstrate the concepts.

* Encourage children to make up their own symbol stories and "read" them to you.

Let's walk to the zoo.

See the ducks swim.

The monkeys are swinging in circles.

The snakes are wiggling.

The kangaroos are hopping.

The elephants are stomping down.

The seals are splashing.

The lion roars.

Oh, it's late! We better run home!

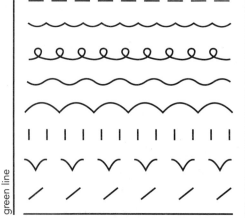

Pointers

Motivate kids to read by using fun tools. All these items make tracking (following lines of print as you read) lots of fun!

Giant Pointer

Fill a cloth garden glove with cotton. With a permanent marker, color fingernails on the glove. Stick a wooden dowel (or cardboard roller from a wire hanger) in the glove and twist it in place with a pipe cleaner. Glue down three fingers and the thumb so the index finger is "pointing." Or simply glue a novelty item (such as a toy, seasonal object, small stuffed animal, and so on) to a dowel.

Magic Pointer

Cover a cardboard roll (from a wire hanger) with aluminum foil or shiny paper. Dip one end in glue, then roll in glitter!

Flyswatter

Cut a rectangle out of a plastic flyswatter and use it to frame words.

Novelty Pencils

Buy playful pencils at a dollar store or party shop. Keep them (unsharpened) in a plastic cup in the reading area and let children choose one when they read.

Eyes on It

Glue a large wiggle eye to the end of a craft stick. Remind children to "keep their eye" on the word as they read!

My Own Magic Wand

Give each child a wooden chopstick. Let them dip one end in glue, then dip it in glitter. Now each child has his or her own magic reading wand!

Witch's Nail

Kids love to wear these nail "caps," which can be purchased around Halloween at a costume or party supply store.

Bugle Reading

You'll certainly capture children's attention with a bag of bugle-shaped corn chips! Show them how to place the chip onto the end of their finger. After reading with the bugle, they can eat it!

Bubble Wand

Bubble wands are perfect for focusing on letters and punctuation. (It's also fun to use them on the overhead.)

Magnifying Glass

Let children bend a pipe cleaner in the shape of a magnifying glass and use it to "examine" words.

Do You Remember?

Help children develop visual memory skills as they focus on environmental print.

Materials: empty cereal (or any other food) boxes in the same size, scissors

How To:

1. Cut the front and backs off the boxes. Mix up the pieces, lay them out on the floor, and have children match the ones that belong together.

2. Next, place the pieces on the floor facedown. Play Concentration. Turn over two at a time. If they match, the player may keep them. If they don't match, the player turns them over and the next player has a turn to match a pair.

3. Continue until all the boxes are matched.

And...

* Start with five pairs, then add more as children become confident.

* Either select boxes that are the same size, or trim boxes so pieces are similar. Individual serving size boxes of cereal also work well.

* Play Concentration with regular playing cards. Start with a few pairs, then add more to challenge children.

* Place four objects on a table. Tell children to look at them and name the objects in order. Have them close their eyes as you remove an object. Can they identify the missing object? You can do the same with felt pieces on a flannel board.

* Cut poster board into 24 four- by six-inch pieces. Draw different shapes on the cards, such as squares, triangles, rectangles, and circles. Make six cards of each shape. Color shapes on two of the cards like colors so you will have 12 pairs. Pass out a shape card to each child, and then have children walk around the room and find the friend whose card matches theirs.

* With index cards, create a memory game with upper- and lowercase letters, mother and baby animals, number words and numerals, and so on.

* Purchase a set of uppercase letter magnets and lowercase letter magnets and have children find pairs.

We're Reading!

Teach children various decoding strategies such as chunking, blending sounds, using picture clues and context, and recognizing sight words—and watch reading confidence soar!

Rime Time

Try any of these ideas (pages 33–34) to help children manipulate letters and make new words. Young children can manipulate only two "chunks" of information at a time in their brain. That's why word family "chunking" is such a powerful decoding strategy for beginning readers.

Egg Words

Write onsets (beginning sounds such as *b*, *c*, *th*, *fl*, *r*, and so on) on the left half of a take-apart plastic egg (the kind found in Easter baskets). Write a rime (a phonogram such as *at*) on the other half. Children rotate the left half and read the words they are forming.

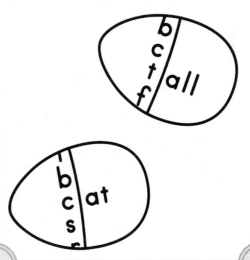

Word Blocks

Gather square and rectangular blocks. Using sticky notes, write onsets on the squares and rimes on the rectangles and stick them to the blocks. Children can manipulate the blocks to make words.

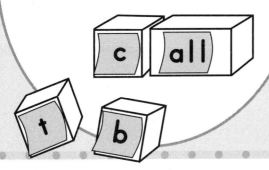

Word Family Wheels

Cut a pie-piece section out of a paper plate. Write a rime on the plate and use a brad fastener to attach it to a second plate. On the second plate, write onsets so that the wheel makes new words as you turn the top plate around.

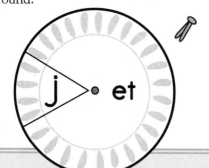

Fold a Word

Fold over sentence strips about two inches from the left end, as shown. Write a word on the strip, then fold over the top section and write another letter that can begin that word. Children open and close the flap, reading the new words.

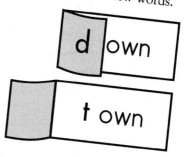

Word Family Flip Book

Cut through all the cards in a spiral-bound index card notebook. Write consonants, blends, and digraphs on the left section, and rimes on the right section. Challenge children to form real (or even nonsense) words!

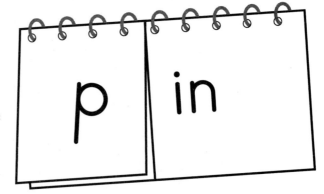

Words, Words, Words!

Provide children with multiple opportunities to master high-frequency words (sight words) or theme-related vocabulary with any of these activities (pages 35–36).

Decoding Detectives

Explicitly model decoding strategies as you share books with the group.

Materials: big books

How To:

When reading aloud, narrate effective reading strategies. For instance, you might say:

- "When I don't know a word, sometimes I look at the picture. Let's look at this picture and see if we can figure out what the word is."

- "I also look at the letters. Let's say them together slowly as we make the sounds."

- "Sometimes I skip over the word I don't know, then I come back when I've finished the sentence and fill in a word that makes sense. Let's try it."

And...

✳ When a child reads a word successfully, ask, *How did you know that?* Encourage him or her to "think out loud" to share how he or she decodes new words.

✳ Make a list on chart paper called "What Do Good Readers Do?" Have children brainstorm and suggest what to do when they come to a word they don't know.

✳ Cover up words in big books with sticky notes and challenge children to guess what the word is, using context clues. Reveal one letter at a time to help them refine their guesses.

Buggy Words

Write sight words on paper cut into bug shapes, and tape the "bugs" to a wall. Children love to "swat" the words with a flyswatter as they read them!

Screen Saver

Display words on your computer screen so that it provides environmental print even when children are not using it!

Red Rover

Write words on index cards and give each child a card to hold. Divide the group into two teams and have them face each other, showing their cards. Teams take turns saying, "Red rover, red rover, send (*word*) right over."

Wear a Word

Cut a piece of paper to fit a clear, pin-on name badge. Choose a different word to wear in the name badge each day. Let children "wear words" as well!

Shout It Out

Sing this to the tune of "If You're Happy and You Know It": "If you can read this word, shout it out…" (or sing it out, whisper it out, and so on).

Spotlight on Words

Turn off the lights, shine a flashlight on a word somewhere in the room, and invite children to read the word.

cat

Mystery Word

Build sound-symbol awareness as children become letter detectives.

Materials: business envelope, sentence strips cut into eight-inch segments, markers

How To:

1. Seal the envelope, then cut off the left side. Write sight words on the sentence strips. Add a picture clue if you like. Insert the sentence strips in the envelope.

2. Explain that you have a mystery word in the envelope and children will have to be "letter-sound detectives" to solve it.

3. Pull out the top strip so the first letter is showing. Ask, *What sound does this letter make? What do you think the word could be?* Reveal the next letter in the word and blend the two sounds together. *Now what do you think it could be?*

4. Continue showing one letter at a time, encouraging children to blend the sounds. When a child guesses correctly, show the entire word and illustration.

And...

✳ Try this with children's names (write "Mystery Friend" on the envelope).

✳ Use the print around the classroom to play the "mystery word" game: "I spy a word that begins with /m/ and ends with /t/." Or, "Who can find a word that rhymes with *cat* and starts with /h/?"

Password

Each day, write a word on a sentence strip or sticky note and attach it to the door frame. Every time children leave or enter the classroom, challenge them to read the "password."

Word Aerobics

Spell out words with your body! Stretch arms up high for tall letters, put hands on hips for short letters, touch the ground for letters with a tail. For example: *d* (hands in air), *o* (hands on hips), *g* (touch the ground). You can also clap on consonants and snap on vowels.

Clipboards

Children can use their very own clipboards as they "read and write the room."

Materials: corrugated cardboard cut into 9- by 12-inch rectangles (one per child), butterfly clip (one per child), paper, markers, pencils

How To:

1. Let each child decorate his or her piece of cardboard with markers.

2. Attach a butterfly clip to each one to create individual clipboards.

3. Clip blank paper onto the clipboards and let children walk around the room and write words they can read.

And...

✴ Send children on a word hunt. First, on a blank sheet of paper, write words that are in the room (calendar words, children's names, classroom labels, word wall words, and so on) and copy the page for each child. Children clip their lists to their clipboards, look around the room for the words, then cross off the words when found.

✴ Challenge children to write the letters from A to Z on their clipboards. Can they find a word that begins with each letter somewhere in the classroom?

✴ Have children look for words with one syllable, two syllables, three, and so on.

✴ As a group, walk around the school and record environmental print.

✴ Ask an optician to donate discarded glass frames (without lenses). Children will get a kick out of wearing these as they read and write the room!

Eating & Reading

Use high-interest materials to build reading confidence!

Materials: food labels, two index cards, markers, self-sealing bag

How To:

1. Ask children to bring in food labels from foods they like.

2. Write "I" on one index card and "like" on the other.

3. Place the cards in a pocket chart and read them together. One at a time, have children place their food label after the words "I like" and read the sentence.

And...

✴ Encourage children to exchange food labels with their friends and read each other's labels.

We're Reading!

Rhythm & Rhyme

Nursery rhymes are rich with opportunities to build phonemic awareness and a love of wordplay. Use traditional nursery rhymes to extend literacy skills with these motivating activities (pages 39–40).

Choral Reading and Singing

Write rhymes on chart paper, the overhead, or a pocket chart. Let children take turns pointing to the words as you read together.

Charades

Have children act out rhymes as their classmates guess which nursery rhyme they are enacting.

Nursery Rhyme Party

Have each child memorize and practice reciting one rhyme. Invite families or another class to a party at which children stand up and recite their special rhyme. Serve Humpty Dumpty egg salad sandwiches, Muffin Man muffins, Jack Horner's pizza, or the Little Teapot's tea!

Dramatizations

Let children act out rhymes as you read them aloud.

Move It!

Invite children to clap, snap, slap thighs, stomp feet, march, hop, patty-cake with a friend, and make other movements as they say or sing rhymes.

Same Song, Different Tune

Did you know that most nursery rhymes can be sung to the tune of "100 Bottles of Pop on the Wall" or "Yankee Doodle"? Try it and see!

Mother Goose Big Book

Let each child illustrate his or her favorite nursery rhyme. Put the picture on a large sheet of paper or a side of a paper grocery sack, along with the words. Make a cover, then bind all the pages together with a book ring. Read the rhymes together during circle time.

Silly Versions

Try some different voices and styles to add a little humor to the nursery rhymes.

Opera Style: Dramatically sing the words and stretch out the sounds like an opera singer!

Rock and Roll: Pretend to hold your guitar as you dance and sing.

With a Cold: Hold your nose as you sing.

Backward: Turn around and face the back of the room as you sing or say rhymes.

Mouse Style: Whisper rhymes with a high, soft voice.

Monster Style: Say rhymes in a loud, gruff voice.

Tape It!

Make a class tape of children singing and saying the rhymes. Use it in your listening center, or let one child take the tape home each evening and share it with his or her family. (You might also reproduce a copy of the tape for each family to use at home.)

Mother Goose's Jukebox

Write rhymes on discarded CDs (the kind you get in the mail and throw in the trash) or make your own CDs from cardboard circles. Write the title of a nursery rhyme on one side of the CD and its text on the other. Cover a cereal box with paper and decorate it with "Mother Goose's Jukebox." Place the CDs in the box. When you need a transition activity, give a child a pretend quarter and say, "Put your quarter in the jukebox and pull out a rhyme." Then read aloud the selected rhyme.

Bookmaking

Bookmaking

If they make it, they will read it! Kids love creating their own books, telling their own stories, and sharing them with others. It's a great way to motivate them to read.

The Book Shop

Don't throw it away! There are so many things you can recycle into books. With all these inviting formats, children will be motivated to read the same books again and again.

Sentence Strip Book

Write simple, emergent-reader-type sentences on six sentence strips and have children illustrate them. Hole-punch each on the left and bind with a book ring. Encourage children to "sweep" their fingers from left to right as they read.

Envelope Book

Write a word or sentence on the front of an envelope and slip a corresponding picture inside. Hole-punch several of these together and bind with string or a metal ring. Children can also write their names on the outside, then place their photo on the inside, or you can write math facts or word problems on the front and put the answers inside.

Collaborative Books

Whenever you create a class collaborative book, you are building reading motivation and confidence, developing print awareness, and also helping to create a sense of class community. Try some of these ideas (pages 42–44) for whole-group reading experiences!

Materials: You can use almost anything for a cover and pages: construction paper, lunch sacks, greeting cards, self-sealing clear bags, Mylar balloons, gift bags, cereal boxes—the possibilities are endless! Some favorite topics for collaborative books:

The Best Thing About Me
Our Wish Book
Family Celebrations
When I Grow Up
If I Were in Charge of the World
Things That Bug Us/Scare Us
My Worst/Best Day Ever
What Does the Principal Do All Day?
I Like…
If I Were the Teacher I Would…
I Can…
We Would Like to Tell the President…
I Know…
If Shoes Could Talk

Consider these elements:

Dedication: Encourage children to dedicate books they make.

Copyright Date: Record the date you make your book.

Publisher: Add your school, city, and state (or, make up a name for your own "publishing company").

Authors and Illustrators: Have children sign a page as authors and illustrators of the book.

ISBN: Include an ISBN number and bar code on the back of your book, just like a real book! Explain to children that these are used by book stores to keep track of books and to tell the price.

The End: Include a page with two words that everybody can read—"THE END!"

Comments & Compliments: Children can take turns bringing the book home for one night. Families can then write their thoughts about the book on a "Comments & Compliments" page.

And…

❋ Older children might do a table of contents, index, or glossary.

❋ Donate the book to your class library, school library, public library, hospital, and so on.

❋ Have a "drawing" at the end of the year so each child gets to keep one of the books.

Baggie Book

Cut construction paper to fit a clear, self-sealing plastic bag. Glue a picture to the paper, label it, then slip it in the bag. Make several of these, then poke holes in one side of the pile and bind the bags together with pipe cleaners. You can place any flat objects in the bags: photos, stamps, leaves, and so on. Write on the bags with permanent marker.

Cracker Jack Book

Cut the front and back off a box of Cracker Jacks. Cut paper the size of the box and give each child a piece to draw a picture of what he or she would like to find for a prize. Punch a hole in the upper left corner and fasten with a pipe cleaner.

Lunch Sack Book

Take four or five lunch sacks and fold up the bottom of each. Staple the open ends of the bags together as shown. Glue a picture so that half of it is hidden under the flap. Children guess what it could be, then lift the flap. You can make other books from this format using riddles, words and pictures, children's names, and so on. Bind sacks with a metal binder ring.

Gift Bag Book

Card shops sell fun, seasonal gift bags. Cut the handle, then the front and back, off of a gift bag. Cut paper the size of the bag and place between the back and front covers. Staple, then punch two holes at the top and reattach handle.

Balloon Book

Deflate a Mylar balloon and laminate it. Cut a back cover the size and shape of the balloon from poster board. Cut newsprint for pages in the book. Punch holes at the top and tie with a ribbon. These are great to make on children's birthdays! Each child can make a page for the birthday boy or girl.

Animal Cookie Book

Cut the front and back off a box of animal cookies. Cut paper the size of the box and place inside. Punch holes at the top and reattach the string handle. Each page might feature a different zoo animal!

Class Phone Book

Remove the front and back covers from an old telephone book. Have each child use one sheet of paper to draw his or her picture and write his or her name, phone number, and address. Place the pages between the front and back cover and bind. Let children pretend to call their friends as they match up numbers on a play telephone, or write letters to each other. This is a great addition to your dramatic play, writing, or math center!

Read & Write

Use any of these bookmaking ideas (pages 45–46) to extend literature. You'll be integrating reading and writing, increasing children's interest in print, and giving children a sense of ownership.

Materials: For all these books, you'll need plain paper or colored paper, pencils, markers, crayons, colored pencils, and other writing materials, plus whatever is specified below.

Snip-Snap Book

1. Make a stack of three sheets of paper and fold the stack in half.

2. Make tears (or snips) about a half inch apart down the fold. Bend one tab forward, then the next backward, and so on, to bind the pages together. Use them for journals, ABC books, original stories, lists of new words, lists of word families, and more.

Brochures

Fold a sheet of paper into thirds to create a brochure. You can use these brochures to illustrate anything that has three "pieces": story elements (beginning, middle, end); letters (capital, lowercase, pictures); letters with lines, curves, or lines *and* curves; or words sorted into lists (two-letter, three-letter, four-letter).

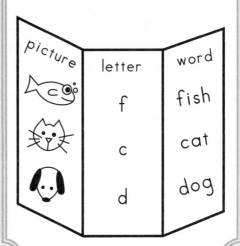

Step Book

Layer two sheets of paper about one inch apart as shown. Fold backward to create a step book with four layers. Staple at fold. Children can create books about four seasons, four steps in cooking, or doing an art project. You can use more sheets of paper to create books with six, eight, or ten pages (for colors in the rainbow, the five senses, days in the week, and so on).

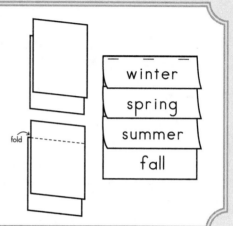

fold

winter
spring
summer
fall

Flip Book

Children like to call this a "garage door" book!

1. With one sheet of paper, make a hot dog fold. (*Fold in half lengthwise.*)

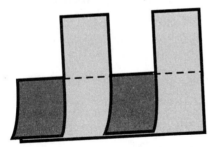

2. Cut as shown to make four flaps.

3. You can use this format for so many things: letters and pictures that begin with the same sound, opposites, before and after, adult and baby animals, sequence of the day, riddles or questions and answers, four seasons, animals and their homes, and so on.

House Book

1. Fold a square sheet of paper in half, crease, and open. Bring upper left corner to the center. Bring upper right corner to the center. Fold up the bottom edge to make a house.

2. Inside, children can write their address, draw pictures of their families, write words they can read around their house (such as "milk" on a carton in the refrigerator), even lists of word "families"!

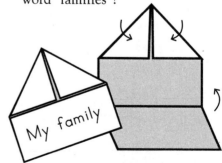

My family

Scrap Bag

These "book bags" are great for assessment purposes —and kids love to show off an "armful" of learning at the end of the year!

Materials: large paper grocery sacks (ten per child for the whole year); crayons, markers, and other art supplies; hole punch; yarn, string, or metal binder rings

How To:

1. At the beginning of each month, give each child a grocery sack and have him or her decorate it with a self-portrait and his or her name. Help children add the name of the month.

2. As children complete projects during the month, have them file their work in the sacks. They might add self-portraits, writing samples, drawings, photos, anecdotal records, lists of books read, reading logs, cutting and pasting samples, journal entries, and so on. Encourage children to add work they are proud of.

3. At the end of the year, give each child a blank sack to decorate for a cover. They can add a photograph of themselves. Put the sacks in order, hole-punch, and tie them together with string or yarn (or metal binder rings).

And...

✳ Store paper sacks in a plastic milk crate or box, open end up. Print each child's name at the top and file alphabetically. Use a date stamp to date work.

✳ Use these bags for parent conferences throughout the year, and share the giant book with families at the end of the year!

✳ You can also use clasp envelopes or large self-sealing bags to make portfolios. Simply have children decorate the covers and save samples each month in these. At the end of the year, punch holes and fasten with book rings or string.

Poetry Songbook

Build a love of language, reading fluency, and awareness of rhyme and rhythm as you create handmade poetry books.

Materials: three-ring binder or pocket folder; copies of songs, nursery rhymes, finger plays, poems, jump rope rhymes, chants, and so on; crayons, markers, and other art supplies

How To:

1. Let children decorate their binders with markers, crayons, and other art materials. Each week, distribute copies (one per child) of a favorite song, poem, or rhyme that relates to a classroom theme.

2. After singing or saying the poem aloud, tell children that you have a copy of the song just for them so they can save it in their poetry songbooks. Distribute copies to children and have them point to the words as you sing together.

3. Have children decorate their pages, then hole-punch and put them in their binders. Use the books during the week for shared reading, guided reading, and independent reading.

And...

* Children can take their songbooks home and read or sing to their families.

Book Boxes

Let children decorate boxes for personal libraries in which they can store their handmade books. They can take these home over the weekend or school vacation, then at the end of the year, so they'll always have a book to read! You can even spray-paint gold or silver and decorate with glitter to make "treasure book boxes."

Little Books

Lay four to six pieces of paper on top of each other. Staple the four corners. Cut into fourths, and you'll have four little books! These are great for picture/word pages (children draw an apple and write *Aa* on one little page, and so on).

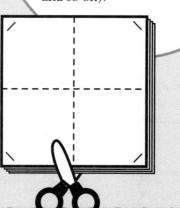